Everything You Need To Know About

GROWING UP
FEMALE

Your female friends can be a great source of support for you as you
grow up.

Everything You Need To Know About

GROWING UP
FEMALE

Ellen Kahaner

Series Editor: Evan Stark, Ph.D.

THE ROSEN PUBLISHING GROUP, INC.
NEW YORK

Published in 1991 by The Rosen Publishing Group, Inc.
29 East 21st Street, New York, New York 10010

First Edition
Copyright © 1991 by The Rosen Publishing Group, Inc.

Library of Congress Cataloging-in-Publication Data

Kahaner, Ellen.
    Everything you need to know about growing up female/Ellen
    Kahaner.—1st ed.
    (The Need to know library)
    Includes bibliographical references and index.
    Summary: Discusses the changes that occur during female
adolescence.
    ISBN 0-8239-1218-3
    1. Teenage girls—United States—Juvenile literature. 2. Young
women—United States—Juvenile literature. 3. Puberty—United
States—Juvenile literature. [1. Adolescent girls. 2. Puberty.
3. Sex instruction for girls.] I. Title. II. Series.
HO786.K27   1991
305.23′5—dc20   90-27470
                                                            CIP
                                                            AC

Contents

Introduction

"**G**rowing up female" is another way to say "becoming a woman." Growing up is a time of many changes, for males as well as for females. You may be worried about the changes you are going through or the changes you know are ahead of you. The more you know, the less you will be worried. That is what this book is about.

What it means to be a woman has not always been the same. Females did not always have the same rights and expectations for their lives that males did. Young women today can look forward to many opportunities in life. These opportunities were won by the efforts of women *and* men who were willing to fight for them. Fighting for the rights of women is called "feminism." It has been a powerful force for change.

Since the 1960s the world has changed a great deal. It is still changing. Until then, most girls were expected to grow up to be wives and mothers. A man was expected to earn the money to support a family.

Today most young women assume that they will get a job when they finish school. Women no longer assume that they will not work after they are married.

Most young women can now look forward to as much schooling as young men. They can look forward to holding any job that a young man can hold. If a young girl wants to become a firefighter, a police officer, or a construction worker, she can do so if she is able to do the work. If a young girl wants to become a dentist, a business executive, or a member of the armed forces, she can do so. A young woman who is willing to study hard and work long hours can prepare for just about any career.

Many young women look forward to being married and having a family. They know that they will probably have to work too. They have a right to expect that a husband will share the responsibilities of keeping a home. They have a right to assume that a man will share the responsibilities of caring for children.

Young women today can learn everything they need to know about their bodies and how to keep them healthy and fit. They can decide when they are ready to have sex. They can decide when they are ready to have children. They can decide what kind of life they most want to live.

This book is for all young people who want to learn what "growing up female" is all about.

Talking to an older sister or friend can help you understand the changes you are going through.

Chapter 1

Growing Up
Means Changing

Mary

"When we were both thirteen, my best friend Katie got pregnant. I looked at her and thought, 'How did this happen? One day we were playing with dolls, and the next . . .' My friends and I thought the changes we were going through were some kind of mystery. We giggled about it. Nobody really knew anything. Then Katie got pregnant. That was when I knew I had to find out some facts."

This book tells about things that happen to teenagers. It gives facts to help you understand what is going on during your teen years. The

9

years between the ages of nine and sixteen years old are known as puberty. Adults who haven't seen you for a while notice that you have changed. They say, "I didn't recognize you! You're a young woman now!" This may surprise you. Is it that easy to see? You are changing inside, too. You may be having many new feelings. Are other girls (and boys) feeling these things too?

Note: The "you" in this book is directed to girl readers. But boys may want to read this book. They may want to find out about how girls feel, too. Then they can understand what is happening to all their friends.

Is puberty really so different for girls and boys? Boys, too, experience very dramatic changes in their bodies. Many things about boys and girls are different. But many things are the same. Sometimes the differences seem more important than they really are. That may happen at school, in the books you read, and in the TV programs you watch.

For example, girls are often shown as boy-crazy and not interested in school. Boys are shown as interested only in sports, math, and science. They are not supposed to show their feelings. Seeing these pictures over and over has a strong effect on you. You get a very limited picture of what girls and boys are really like. Then, if you don't fit into that picture, you may feel different. You may feel that something is wrong with you.

Boys and girls have a lot more in common than most people think. For instance, both girls and boys need friends to survive this hard time of life.

Everyone reacts in their own way to the physical, emotional, and psychological changes of puberty. As your body grows, it changes *physically*. You look different. Your body changes slowly for several years. Your *emotions* (feelings) change because of what is going on in your body. The people around you and the things that happen to you affect your feelings, too. *Psychological* changes affect your personality: who you are, what you think, and what is important to you.

Some of these changes are very different for girls and boys. Different doesn't mean better or worse—just "not the same." This book will help you understand the reasons for the changes, and the reasons for your reactions to them.

Chandra
"Until this year, I looked like a telephone pole. My mother called me 'Miss Skinny.' I never thought I'd look pretty. Then, all of a sudden, I got curves. I'd look in the mirror and not recognize myself. It was kind of exciting."

That is an example of physical change. The many changes in your body during puberty are dramatic. People change at different rates, and at different ages. The average age at which girls start menstruating (having periods) is twelve or thirteen. But some girls start as early as nine. Some don't start until sixteen.

Carmen
"I still thought I was a kid. Then all of a sudden other people didn't think so. My best friend and I went trick-or-treating in our neighborhood. People greeted us at the door saying, 'You're too old to trick-or-treat.' It freaked me out."

That is an emotional change. Sometimes you seem to be on an emotional roller coaster. Your feelings change all the time. How do you handle all the changes? You may want to be treated differently. But you may also want to be treated the same as always. Your parents may not treat you the way you want to be treated. Your teachers may not want to know about what you are going through. That is why it is important to have friends. You can share with them when you are feeling and doing things for the first time. You need to know that someone understands how you feel. A friend can make all the difference.

Beth

"*My mother and I always went shopping for clothes together. We had the same tastes. Then I started wanting to wear different kinds of clothes. I wanted to go shopping with my friends. I didn't want to hurt my mother's feelings. But I really wanted to be on my own.*"

That is an example of psychological change. Your personality is formed by what happens to you in your family and in the world around you. What happens to you now—at home, at school, with friends, dating—affects your personality. These relationships will help to shape the person you are becoming.

Too many people grow up doing what is expected of them. They don't learn to think for themselves. For example, if John's father has a grocery store, it may be expected that John will own it one day. If Beth's mother is a housewife, Beth will be a housewife. The forces directing you to repeat your father's or mother's life can be very strong.

You may admire your mother, and want to be just like her. But it is also very natural to want to do your own thing. You need to think seriously about *your own* values and desires. The decisions you make between the ages of nine and sixteen have a lot to do with how you shape your life as an adult.

Everyone grows at a different rate during puberty. Some girls get tall in one big spurt, others need a little longer.

Chapter 2

Body Changes

Chandra

"I was always average in height, but it seemed like overnight I was turning into a giant. My feet were already a size 9 when I was in seventh grade. My arms and legs looked twice as long as the rest of my body. My clothes didn't fit, and my feet hung over the foot of my bed. I started to feel like the Jolly Green Giant."

Your body starts to grow faster during puberty. Hormones cause these changes. Teenagers have strong and active hormones. This rapid growth is called a "growth spurt." It lasts about a year. Usually the growth spurt happens before your breasts develop and before pubic hair starts to grow.

15

The average girl grows two inches a year
from age two until puberty. By the time you've
had your first menstrual period, your growth
rate usually slows down. Most girls reach their
adult height within one to three years after their
first period.

Boys also have a growth spurt during puberty, but theirs begins a couple of years later
than girls'. That's why girls at eleven and
twelve are often taller than boys the same age.
By the age of thirteen or fourteen, boys catch
up and often grow taller than most girls.

A growth spurt is only one of the *many*
changes during puberty. The shape of your face
changes. The lower part lengthens and your
face gets fuller. The shape of your body
changes gradually. You may not even notice it
at first.

Your body weight is rearranged. Fat tissue
grows around your hips, thighs, and buttocks,
giving you a curvier shape. Your breasts, vagina, uterus, and ovaries grow. All of these
changes are caused by hormones. Your body
changes the most around the time you begin to
menstruate. When you begin to menstruate
(have your period) you are capable of having a
baby. That is a very important change. But it
is not a change that others will be able to notice
by looking at you. You will learn more about
the changes inside your body in Chapter 3.

You are probably concerned about the changes you are going through that *can* be seen by other people. Let's look at some of those changes a little more closely.

One of the changes is the growth of your breasts. Each girl's rate of growth is different. If your breasts grow when you are eleven or twelve, that is normal for you. If they do not grow until you are fifteen, that is also normal.

You may worry that your breasts are too large, or too small. It is not a good idea to compare yourself to others. Everyone's shape is different. You may notice that your two breasts are not the same size, or even exactly the same shape. That is because each person's left and right sides are slightly different.

Some girls want to wear a bra when their breasts begin to grow. That may not be necessary, but you should do what makes you feel comfortable. If you play active sports or do strenuous exercise, a bra is a good idea. Special bras are made for that purpose.

From time to time you may notice that your breasts are tender or hurt. The tenderness usually lasts only a day or two, usually before your period. It is normal.

Hair starts to grow under your arms and around your genital area where your legs come together. The hair on your legs grows thicker and may be darker.

You begin to sweat more because your sweat glands are more active. You will notice that your sweat has an odor. This odor can be very strong and unpleasant. You can avoid body odor by showering or bathing often. You may also use a deodorant or an antiperspirant.

Your hormones control your glands. The oil glands in your body are more active too. Active oil glands can cause greasy hair. You may need to wash your hair every day. Active oil glands can also cause skin problems. Pimples—blackheads and whiteheads—form in pores in which oil is trapped. Acne begins the same way. This skin condition can get bad enough to need a doctor's care.

Some young people have serious skin problems. Some have mild skin problems, and some have none at all. But all young people should take good care of their skin. You should wash your face with a mild soap or use a skin cleanser every morning and every night.

All these changes have a strong effect on how you feel about yourself. It helps to talk to your friends about what is happening. You'll find that others are going through the same kinds of things. How are *they* coping? Sharing experiences will help you feel better.

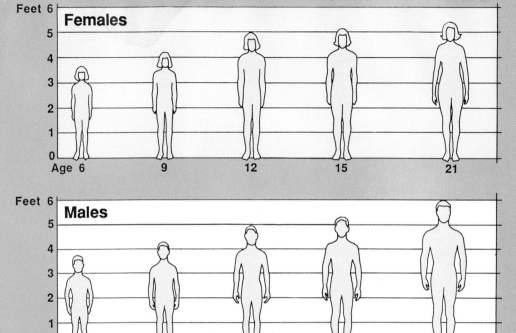

Boys Are Changing Too

Boys start to change when they are a little older, but they too go through many changes during puberty. Besides growing taller and developing more strength and muscle tone, there are other changes.

Some changes boys go through are obvious, like those girls go through. Boys grow body hair too—under their arms, in the genital area, on their legs. Boys sweat a lot too. Boys can have skin problems just as well as girls.

Some changes boys go through are not obvious. Just as girls experience changes in their genital organs, so do boys. These changes mean the same for boys as for girls. They become capable of reproducing—making a baby.

19

Menstruation is a dramatic change in your body that signals your
young adulthood.

Chapter 3

About Girls' Menstruation

The beginning of menstruation is the most dramatic change in a young woman's body during puberty. Menstruation is also referred to as "having your period." When a young woman begins to menstruate, she is capable of reproducing. She can become pregnant and have a baby. Chapter 4 explains what happens to your body during pregnancy. But first you must understand menstruation.

The word "menstruation" comes from a Latin word that means "month." That is because a woman menstruates every month. The cycle of hormone activity that ends with menstruation takes about 28 days in most women.

Girls begin menstruating between the ages of nine and eighteen. For the next 40 years or so, you will get your period every 21 to 40 days. There are some exceptions. You may not have a period if:

- You are pregnant.
- You are nursing a baby.
- You are very underweight.
- You are sick.
- You are having problems with your reproductive system.

You may or may not have your period at the same time each month. It may take your body some time, even a year or more, to get into a regular pattern.

Many years ago people didn't know what caused menstruation. Stories were made up about menstruating women. The stories were based on fear, not facts. But even today some people think something is different about a girl or a woman when she has her period. Menstruation is your body's natural way of cleaning itself. Having your period is normal and healthy.

Carmen
"It was at night. My older sisters and I were watching "Growing Pains" on TV. I was twelve. My parents were at the movies. All of a sudden

my head started to hurt. I had a bad stomach-ache. I went into the bathroom and saw red stains on my underpants. I got scared and called my sisters. They talked to me through the bathroom door. They were really excited. Then I got excited. I couldn't believe it was happening to me. I felt grown-up. The next day when I got home from school there were little presents on my bed. It was like a party."

Older sisters, a friend, your mother, or an aunt can give you facts about menstruation. Some schools have special classes for girls about menstruation. But often girls get too few facts, and too late. Some girls are not prepared when they have their first period. They have not been told what will happen. They don't know what to do.

Mary

"I was really young when I got my period, about nine and a half. None of the girls in my class had it yet. I was at school. Someone said, 'There's blood on the back of your jeans.' I got scared and started to cry. I told my teacher. She went with me to the nurse's office. Later when I told my mother, her face got red. She handed me a book and said, 'Look it up.' She wouldn't even say the word. For a long time I really hated getting my period."

THE MENSTRUAL CYCLE

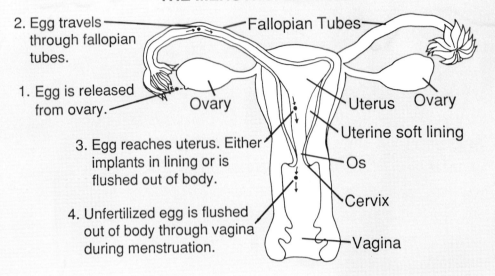

2. Egg travels through fallopian tubes.

1. Egg is released from ovary.

Ovary

Fallopian Tubes

Uterus   Ovary

Uterine soft lining

3. Egg reaches uterus. Either implants in lining or is flushed out of body.

Os

Cervix

4. Unfertilized egg is flushed out of body through vagina during menstruation.

Vagina

What is your menstrual cycle? It begins the first day of your period. It is usually 28 days.

Your menstrual cycle has two purposes:

- To prepare your uterus to help a baby grow if you become pregnant.
- To clean out the uterus if pregnancy does not happen.

Your menstrual cycle includes:

- The making of special hormones
- The thickening of the uterine lining
- Ovulation
- The breakdown of the uterine lining
- Menstruation (bleeding).

It is helpful to know about the body organs that are part of the menstrual cycle and reproductive process.

Cervix—lower narrow end of the uterus that juts into the vagina.

Fallopian tubes—tubes at top of uterus that carry one ripe egg to the uterus each month.

Follicle—a tiny pocket in the ovary where the egg ripens.

Hormones—chemical substances that travel in your blood and tell your body organs how to develop. Your body makes hundreds of hormones. Estrogen and progesterone are the hormones that control the menstrual cycle.

Os—opening to the uterus.

Ovaries—organs that provide safe storage for the thousands of eggs you were born with. Each ovary is about the size and shape of an almond.

Pituitary gland—small oval gland near the brain.

Uterus—hollow organ that grows during puberty to the size of a clenched fist. The uterus can expand to many times its size. The baby grows there.

On the fifth day after your cycle begins, the pituitary gland sends a signal to your ovaries. The "signal" is carried by hormones to the eggs in your ovaries. Only one egg matures or ripens and is released during each menstrual cycle. At the same time, the ovary sends out estrogen and signals your uterine lining to become thicker with blood and tissue.

On or about the fourteenth day of your cycle, you ovulate. A ripe egg breaks out of its follicle and rises to the top of your ovary. You may feel a cramp when the ripe egg pops off the ovary.

The fallopian tube has fringed ends. These ends draw the egg into the tube, and carry it to the uterus. Meanwhile, the broken follicle makes the hormone progesterone. Progesterone causes the uterine lining to become even thicker. If the egg is not fertilized (if you have not become pregnant), the egg breaks down. The estrogen and progesterone give signals to your uterus. The lining of the uterus starts to break up by about day 24.

By day 28, the uterine lining has loosened so much that it breaks off and begins to come out of your cervix and vagina. The beginning of menstruation (bleeding) is called day 1.

What comes out of your vagina is usually called "blood" because it is red. But it is really a mixture of tissue, mucus, and blood. Some blood is lost, but not much.

Cramps are caused by muscles in your uterus. The muscles tighten up to push the menstrual fluid out. Cramps are also caused when the muscles of your cervix open the os a little to let the fluid out.

Cramps are a physical symptom (sign) that you have when you are menstruating. But your body is experiencing changes during the entire menstrual cycle. Not all young women experience menstruation in the same way. Just as our physical bodies are different, they work in different ways.

Having your period is not always easy. Sometimes it means dealing with cramps, headaches, and mood swings.

Some young women have a short cycle (26 days or less) and some have a long cycle (30 days or more). Some young women experience bleeding for only two or three days. Some have their period for a week or even longer. Some women have a heavy flow (they "bleed" a lot) for a day or two and less flow for a few other days. Some bleed very little. Some women have cramps with every period. Some never have cramps at all.

Most women do not change their activities when they have their periods. They go to school or work, do moderate exercise, and play sports. Exercise can help to lessen cramps and make you feel better. Some young women do have pain. It is a good idea to see a doctor about painful menstruation. A doctor who takes care of women is called a gynecologist. But most young women do not need to see a doctor because of problems with menstruation.

Besides menstruation itself, you may go through some physical changes during your cycle. Other changes are emotional and affect your feelings. You may have "mood swings" as you get close to the time for your period. Mood swings are changes in the way you feel. Sometimes the changes are rapid and intense. You may have heard about *premenstrual syndrome* or *PMS.*

PMS is a combination of emotional and physical changes that you can go through just before your period. Mood swings are intense in someone who experiences PMS. You feel very nervous and upset. Other changes in your body can include *bloating* (tissues filling with fluid). This is sometimes called "water weight gain." It usually lasts only for the few days just before your period. Some young women have tenderness in their breasts. Some find that their hair and skin are oilier. Some young women find that their system releases thicker fluid at times between their periods. This mucous secretion is usually colorless and is perfectly normal.

Many women can tell when they are about to get their period even if they don't get their period at the same time every month. They recognize the signs their body sends them.

Not everyone has all of these symptoms. Some women don't have any of them. Some have them sometimes but not always. Women who do get them learn to expect them. They know how to deal with them.

You may be thinking that it would be much easier if you didn't have to have a period every month. That is probably true. But having your period is your body's way of telling you that you are not pregnant. It is also the way your body cleans your reproductive system. And that is very important.

What Do I Use When I Have My Period?

Young women today have many choices. Information about these choices is available everywhere. There are advertisements in women's magazines and even on television. Your mother, sister, friend, or school nurse can tell help you make choices.

Menstrual pads used to be called "sanitary napkins." They are made of paper and other absorbent fibers. Most pads have adhesive strips that attach directly to your panties. Most have a fluid-proof shield inside that protects against leaking and staining. Pads come in many sizes and shapes. Some are thick to protect against heavy flow. These are often called "maxi-pads" by the companies that make them. Some are very thin, to use toward the end of your period or when you think you might get your period. These are often called "mini-pads," or "panty shields." You may want to try different shapes and sizes of pads until you find the one that is best for your needs.

The other kind of protection you can use during your period is called a *tampon*. Tampons are worn inside your body. A tampon is made of paper and other absorbent fibers rolled together. The fibers absorb the flow. Some tampons have a plastic or cardboard applicator. That makes it easier to insert a tampon into the vagina. A tampon has a string attached to it. A portion of the string hangs down just a little below the lips of the vagina. That makes it easy to remove the tampon.

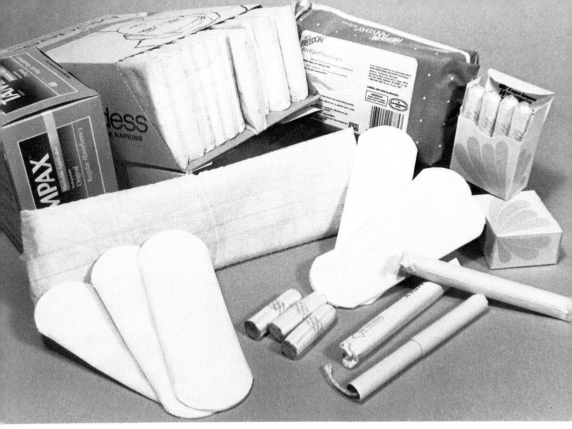

Many products that help with menstruation—such as tampons, panty shields, and maxi-pads—are available in stores.

Tampons come in different sizes and shapes. Many young women find the smaller sizes more comfortable. But everyone's body is different. If you decide to use tampons, try different kinds until you find one you like.

One thing to remember about tampons is *very important.* You must change them often, at least two or three times a day. A very serious disease can be caused by not changing tampons frequently enough. *Toxic shock syndrome* can cause high fever and vomiting. In extreme cases, death can occur.

Whatever you decide to use when you have your period, remember to change frequently. You will feel fresher, and it is important for your health.

Becoming sexually active means you and your partner must think responsibly about birth control.

Chapter 4

Sex and Pregnancy

After the first time you menstruate, you have the ability to reproduce. You can have a baby. That doesn't mean you have to or want to. It means that if and when you want to, you can. You can become pregnant if you have sex during ovulation, or shortly before or after.

Remember, you can ovulate at a different time each month. There are no "safe days" to have sex. *If you do not want to become pregnant, you must always use some form of birth control.*

How Pregnancy Happens

Sperm from a male's body meets the egg from the female's body in one of the fallopian tubes. A sperm breaks through the outer shell of the ripe egg and moves inside it. This is called fertilization. If the egg is fertilized, it attaches itself to the wall of the uterus and pregnancy begins.

For the egg and sperm to unite, sperm must leave the male's body and enter the female's body. Generally, this happens during sexual intercourse, when the penis enters the vagina. It is possible that during foreplay some sperm can leak out and enter the vagina. Foreplay includes kissing, hugging, and touching each other's sexual organs.

When a male has an erection, blood rushes into his penis and fills up the spongy tissue. The muscles at the base of the penis stiffen so that the blood stays in the penis. That makes the penis hard. The hardness allows the penis to enter comfortably into the vagina.

Sperm are released when the muscles of the erect penis contract. The sperm are forced up and out through the urethra, a tube that runs down the middle of the penis. This process is called ejaculation. Another word for it is "orgasm." A slang word for ejaculate is "come."

Millions of sperm are released every time a male ejaculates. After ejaculation the sperm swim to the top of the vagina. They pass through the cervix into the uterus. Some sperm swim into the fallopian tubes. It takes only one of these millions of sperm to fertilize a ripe egg. If a sperm fertilizes the egg, pregnancy begins.

You can learn more about pregnancy from books like *Everything You Need to Know About Teen Pregnancy.* Over one million teenage girls become pregnant every year in the United States alone. Only one out of every five pregnant teenagers *wanted* to have a baby. Some pregnant teenagers don't even know that sex causes pregnancy.

We have talked a lot in this book about learning about your body. We have learned how the female body works and how pregnancy occurs.

Information about sex is important, too. You need to have information in order to make good decisions. You are the only one who can decide whether you are ready to have sex or not.

Don't let yourself be pressured into sexual activity by friends or boyfriends. You may believe that it is important to remain a virgin until you get married. You may feel that having sex is an important part of a relationship whether you are married or not. Some people think it is okay for boys to have sex, but not for girls. That kind of thinking is called a "double standard." Some people call girls who have sex

"sluts." Have you ever heard of a boy being
called a "slut"? Some people think that whatever decision a person makes about sex is right,
as long as the person is responsible. Being
sexually responsible means not doing anything
that can hurt you or your partner, or have a bad
effect on your future. It means having safe sex
by using a birth control device to prevent AIDS
and other sexually transmitted diseases (STD),
and pregnancy.

Don't have sex unless you know how to prevent pregnancy and STD. Remember, too, that
it isn't just *your* responsibility to see that you
don't become pregnant or infected. Birth control and protection against disease is your
partner's responsibility too.

All teenagers have some interest in sex, even
if they are only curious about it. Some teenagers think about sex a lot. Some don't. Some
teenagers are not even ready for dating. That is
okay too. Everyone grows up at her or his own
pace. We all seem to grow up eventually. It is
important to think about what is right for *you.*
Most people are attracted to the opposite sex.
But some are attracted to their own sex. That
is called *homosexuality.* Women who are attracted to other women are called *lesbians.*
People who are attracted to their own sex are
more accepted than they have been in the past.
It is still difficult for some people to understand

FEMALE REPRODUCTIVE SYSTEM

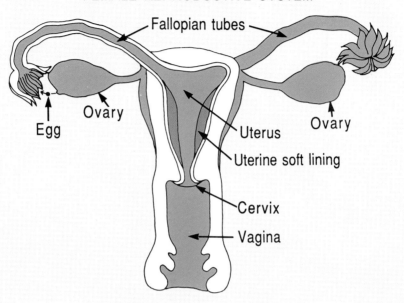

Fallopian tubes

Ovary

Egg

Ovary

Uterus

Uterine soft lining

Cervix

Vagina

MALE REPRODUCTIVE SYSTEM

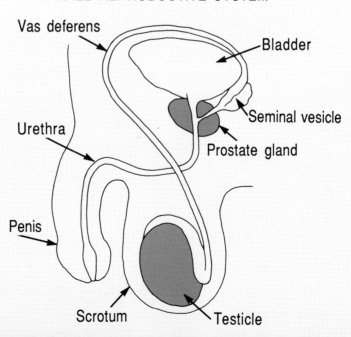

Vas deferens

Bladder

Seminal vesicle

Urethra

Prostate gland

Penis

Scrotum

Testicle

that kind of attraction. But it is important to respect other people's rights and feelings. If you know young people who are homosexual you should not discriminate against them (treat them differently than you treat others).

Most young people explore their bodies and soon discover that touching themselves feels good. This is called *masturbation*. Most young people masturbate. Stimulating yourself for pleasure is normal. Many people do it all their lives, even after they are married.

When people kiss and touch each other's bodies, that is called making out, or petting. When it is done before having sex it is called foreplay. Kissing and petting help the woman's and man's body get ready for sex. It stimulates the man to have an *erection*. His penis fills with blood and becomes stiff. That makes it easy for the penis to enter the woman's vagina. The woman's body also reacts to foreplay. Fluids are released in the vagina that make it smooth so the penis can enter easily. Inside the lips of a woman's vagina is a small organ that is very sensitive. It is called the *clitoris*. It becomes enlarged when a woman is excited by kissing and touching. The clitoris provides the woman's sexual release, or *orgasm*. When it is rubbed it causes spasms that release tension in the woman's body. In sexual intercourse, the man's penis rubs against the clitoris.

Young people sometimes have a hard time remembering that kissing and petting are foreplay. Their bodies are designed to want sex when they are stimulated. That is why it is important to know the facts.

Birth control is easy for young people to obtain if they know the facts. If you decide to have sex and do not want to become pregnant, be responsible and use birth control.

Another factor in deciding about having sex is STD—sexually transmitted disease. You can learn more about this subject in a book such as *Everything You Need to Know about STD*. STD can be very serious. Some sexually transmitted diseases, such as *herpes,* can be treated, but cannot be cured. Others, like AIDS, can kill. You can get them from someone who doesn't look or act ill. You can protect yourself against STD by making sure that you know your partner and his history of sexual behavior. You can insist that your partner wear a *condom.* A condom is a thin rubber sheath that a man rolls up over his penis. It will hold the sperm and fluid inside. You are protected from diseases because of the barrier between you. A condom provides good protection against pregnancy, STD, and AIDS.

Reproduction: Facts and Fiction

Here are some questions and answers about pregnancy and sex.

Question: I heard that you will get pregnant if you get into bed with a guy. Is that true?
Answer: The only way you can get pregnant is by having sexual intercourse without proper birth control.

Question: If you know too much about how the body works, is sex less fun?
Answer: Girls and boys are often afraid to ask about sex or to say what they want. Being honest makes sex (or anything) more fun.

Question: All my friends say you can't get pregnant if you have sex during your period. Are they right?
Answer: Wrong! You can ovulate even during your period. Ovulation does not happen at the same time every month. You *can* get pregnant if you have sex when you have your period.

Question: Everyone says that it is impossible to get pregnant the first time you have sex. Is that true?
Answer: You can get pregnant the first, second, or any time you have sexual contact.

Question: I've been lucky. I don't use birth control, but my boyfriend says he knows when to pull out and not to worry. Is he right?
Answer: It's not a matter of luck. If you have unprotected sex, the odds are very great that you will get pregnant. (Four out of five girls who have unprotected sex get pregnant.)

Question: Isn't birth control a girl's responsibility?
Answer: It is the responsibility of both partners. Teenagers who decide to have sexual intercourse need to talk about the type of birth control they want to use. Leaving the decision to chance is very risky. Both people need to take responsibility for actions that affect their lives.

Question: Isn't it illegal for minors to buy over-the-counter (nonprescription) birth control (such as condoms, foam, and the sponge)?
Answer: No. You can get pamphlets describing all methods of birth control at Planned Parenthood centers and other family planning centers. You can buy condoms at drug stores and at some supermarkets. You can also learn more about birth control from books such as *Everything You Need to Know about Birth Control.* Having the facts will help you and your partner decide what method is best for you as a couple.

Staying active is an important way to help your body develop during your teen years.

Chapter 5

Growing Up Fit

Today girls know that being physically active not only helps your body, but your mind and spirit, too. But old-fashioned ideas keep some girls on the sidelines instead of on the playing field. Let's look at why it is important to keep moving.

Exercise is good for every system in your body: the cardiovascular system (the heart and circulation), the respiratory system (breathing), the musculoskeletal system (muscles), the reproductive system, and your emotions.

Cardiovascular System

The heart gets stronger and works better when you exercise. A regular workout, which means exercising hard for twenty minutes or more (aerobic exercise)—causes the number and size of the blood vessels in your tissues to increase. That causes the blood supply to increase also. When your blood circulates faster,

oxygen and nutrients move to every part of
your body more quickly. Wastes are removed
faster. That is why you usually feel better after
exercising.

Respiratory System

When you exercise, your respiratory system
grows stronger. You take deeper and more
regular breaths. More air enters and leaves
your lungs. Oxygen is needed by every cell in
your body. Your bloodstream carries it from
your lungs.

Musculoskeletal System

Without regular exercise your muscles get
weak and flabby. Strong abdominal (stomach)
muscles don't just make you look good in a
bikini. They keep your lower back from aching.
They help you digest your food. Strong
muscles in your legs improve your circulation
and help you get where you want to go. If your
arms are strong, you will be more independent.
Strong muscles increase bone strength. You'll be
able to carry things and do everyday chores.

Reproductive System

Exercise helps you feel better before and
during your periods. It eases cramps. Staying
active is good for your whole body, including
your uterus and breasts.

Emotions

During puberty the dramatic changes in your body go together with strong feelings. This sometimes causes your muscles to tense. Muscle tension can cause headaches, leg cramps, and stomach aches. You may have trouble breathing, which makes you feel tired. Sometimes exercise can release the tension and can "straighten your head out" as well.

Beth

"After school, I have to pick up my sister at the day-care center, get her settled down, clean up around the house, start dinner, and do my home- work. By the time Mom comes home from work, I'm ready to go to sleep! But if I take a run, I get myself back together. I remember who I am. I think about what I want to do. It gives me a lot of positive energy!"

Exercise is good for you and makes you feel better about yourself. So why is it sometimes so hard to get yourself to exercise? There are forces in your life that can make it hard to move around freely. Some of these are:

• **Money:** Joining a Y or an exercise class costs money. The budget for after school pro- grams is less than ever. If your family is having trouble making ends meet, an exercise program may not be a top priority.

- **Couch potato culture:** TV watching and being driven everywhere you want to go can result in an under-exercised body. The less active you are, the harder it is to think positively about exercising.
- **Prejudiced ideas:** Boys are strong, girls are weak. Sweating is unfeminine. Muscles are ugly on girls. Boys are the athletes, girls the cheerleaders. All too often, girls are taught to believe these negative ideas. Then they accept them as facts.

Try one of these things to get yourself moving:

- **Exercising at home:** That is cheaper than joining a class, and you can do it whenever you want to. You can turn on the radio and dance or stretch, jump rope, or run in place. Look around your town. You may find a public swimming pool, a running track, or tennis courts in a nearby park.
- **Exercise with a friend:** Sometimes it's hard to exercise alone. Try finding an exercise buddy—a friend who wants to run, stretch, or bike ride with you. You are more likely to keep exercising if it's also fun.

It is very important for you to get the exercise you need. You can run, dance, swim, do yoga or karate, or play team sports. A strong body goes along with a strong mind.

Chapter 6

Liking What You See in the Mirror

Mary
"I worry a lot about how I look. The magazine models have perfect bodies, perfect skin and perfect hair. I'm a mess in comparison. I wish I had a different body. Sometimes I think there isn't a single part of me that's fine just the way it is. I'll never match up."

Who defines beauty in our society? Your ideas about beauty come from the magazines you read, the TV programs you watch, and the movies you see. Your parents and friends may also have strong feelings about how you should look. That affects you, too.

Today in our country the ideal beauty is often shown as a thin, tall, white woman wearing lots of makeup and expensive clothes. The image is shown so often that you may believe that is what beauty really is.

Many companies spend huge sums of money on advertising to make even more money selling makeup and beauty products. They want you to think that buying this brand of deodorant or that shampoo will make you happier and more popular. They make you feel that something is wrong with how you look and smell.

Chandra

"When I was younger I did everything I could to have straight hair. One day my mother came into my room and said, 'Think about how much time, energy, and money you spend trying to fit into somebody else's idea of looking good. If you weren't fussing with your hair, what else could you be doing?' It really made me wonder why I was spending all that time on my hair. I mean, was it going to help me get into law school?"

Many girls believe that how they look is as important as who they are. They become totally wrapped up in how they look. It may be fun at times to play around your looks. But it's important to ask who benefits by all the time and money spent seeking "beauty." How is it helping you to grow as a person?

As you mature, your physical appearance will become more important to you.

If you like yourself, you will be able to make your own decisions about clothes, makeup, and beauty products. Decide what food plan to follow based on what *you* want for yourself, not what you think other people want.

Liking yourself takes practice. Try looking in the mirror to see what you like about your looks. Help your friends feel good about themselves too.

Do "the right thing" for yourself. Think about:

Clothes

You are going through physical, emotional, and psychological changes. You may also want to try changing how you dress. Maybe you have always worn blouses neatly tucked into pleated skirts. You may want to try wearing long skirts with loose-fitting tops—neat one day, way-out the next.

Trying different dress styles is part of figuring out who you are. Don't be afraid of making a mistake. If you wear something that doesn't make a fantastic outfit, it's not the end of the world. It may take time to find a style you're comfortable with.

Your idea of how you want to look may clash with your parents' idea. Sometimes talking over how you feel will help. You may not be free to dress the way you want to now, but the time will come when you can.

Your mom can be a good source of advice about clothes, personal hygiene, and makeup.

Makeup

Some girls start wearing makeup at a very young age. Some wait until they are older. Some decide not to use makeup at all.

- "It makes me feel better about how I look."
- "I feel like a painted doll."
- "It's fun."
- "If boys wore makeup I'd feel better about spending my time putting it on."

Those are some of the comments girls make about this subject.

Parents also have different ideas about makeup. Some parents forbid their daughters to use makeup until they are older.

Again, it's a matter of choosing what feels right to you. As with your style of dress, you may go through stages with makeup.

Keep in mind that some cosmetic companies make claims that are untrue. If you have questions about the products, check in the library.

Diet

Most teenage girls think they are overweight. That's because the idea that "thin" is better than "fat" is in the TV programs you watch, the movies you see, and the magazines you read. Your parents may also believe that idea. Many girls worry so much about being fat that they develop serious eating disorders.

The real issue isn't how much you weigh, it's what you eat. Learning to eat in a healthful way is very important.

In the past many girls stopped exercising at puberty, or exercised less, because it was considered "unladylike." Today, being physically active is encouraged. We know it is good for you. It helps to keep your weight in a healthy range. Looking athletic and healthy is popular now. It also helps you work out some of your emotional ups and downs. Exercise is healthier than using food to make yourself feel better.

Does your school offer nutrition classes? Educating yourself about good nutrition will help you develop good eating habits.

Chapter 7

Friendship and Dating

During puberty it is common to spend time with a group of friends. Within that group, one or two may become your best friends. You may also find that you have boys as friends, in a non-romantic way.

Carmen
"I knew Sam since kindergarten. We grew up together. We were always close friends, but when we started to date other people we became even closer. Why? We asked each other for advice and cheered each other up."

Sometimes you may be outside of a group that you want to be "in." You may feel too shy to approach this group, or you may not want to risk rejection. You may feel lonely, scared, and out of it.

Keep in mind that everyone experiences feelings of loneliness and rejection. *Everyone* has feelings of insecurity and shyness at times. That's why going to a party with a friend is easier than going by yourself. You can help each other through it. Also, liking yourself affects how much you like other people. If you don't like yourself, chances are you'll find many reasons to dislike others. You'll find yourself alone a lot.

Dating

What happens when you meet a boy you would like to get to know? Many girls are raised with the idea that they should wait to be asked out. That way they have little control over their own social life.

However, many girls today feel that they don't have to follow rules about the "proper" way to act. That gives you a lot more options. Many boys understand that it's not easy for girls to ask for a date. Boys know what it's like to be rejected, too. The worst thing that will happen if you ask is that you'll get a "no." But at least you've tried. That takes courage.

Going out with boys gives you the chance to explore new relationships.

Sometimes when you go out with a boy you'll find out that you don't really like him. You won't want to date him again. Or you may find that you'd be more comfortable having him as a friend. In both of these cases, it's important to be direct about how you feel.

You may also find that you like the person a lot. You may even fall in love. These relationships can last, but usually not long. Often, during puberty, relationships are short and intense. Each one teaches you a little about yourself and about what kinds of people are best for you.

When you are dating, the question of how far to go sexually will probably arise. Don't be pressured into doing something you don't want to do. If you're not sure, the best thing may be to wait until you are. Try to learn as much as you can about yourself and about relating to others. That way, next time you'll know more about how to act in a relationship and what you like and dislike.

Some people begin dating even before they reach their teens. Others don't date even though they are in high school. You may think you're ready for dating before you have the chance. Don't worry. Your social life takes a while to get started. You have plenty of time.

Chapter 8

Looking Ahead

Mary

"When I was a little kid and someone asked me what I wanted to be when I grew up, I'd say, 'A teenager.' Now that I'm a teenager, it's more scary to think ahead. I want to be an adult, but what does that mean?"

Becoming an adult includes planning and thinking about your future. Your culture may give you a very strong message about what is expected of you when you grow up. Your family may have their own idea of what you're supposed to do. Without planning, "accidents" (like an early pregnancy) can put your life out of control.

You have the right to plan and dream about your future. You may think about people whom you would like to be like, whose life stories you've read about in books or seen in movies. You may know an adult friend you would like as a role model.

In thinking about what you would like to do, be careful of the voice inside that says, "You'll never be able to do that. It's only a pipe dream."

Try one of these suggestions for thinking about your future:

• Try to have experiences outside of what is expected of you. Whether it is getting into a work/study program at your high school, traveling, living with another family—all the experiences you have add up. They give you ideas and choices to use in figuring out what you would like to do.

• Try to make friends with some adults you can talk to about your future. Don't be afraid to talk to other people. Ask for their thoughts and advice. Adults have had different kinds of experiences. They may know about places that are available to help you get to know yourself.

Chandra

"I worked as a summer intern in a law office, through a program at my high school. I got an inside look at what lawyers do, and I earned

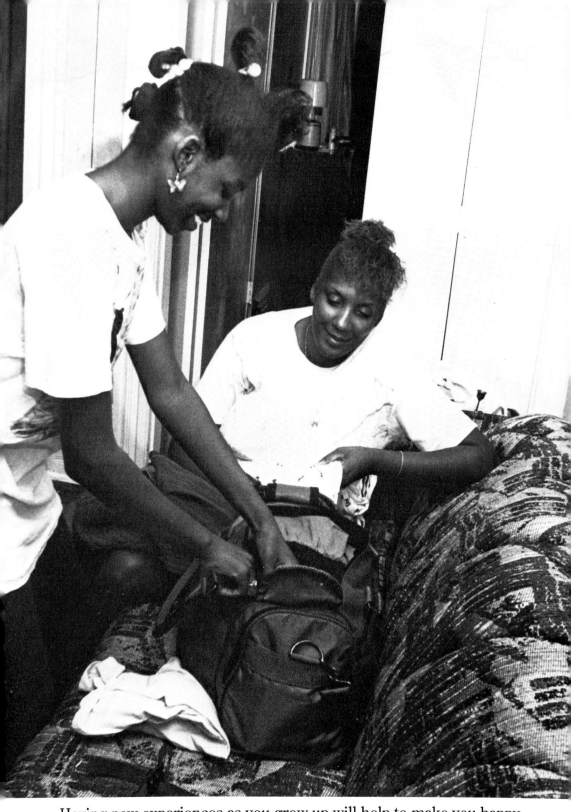

Having new experiences as you grow up will help to make you happy
and confident as an adult.

some credit. I never would have known what it was really like to be a lawyer. I definitely would have thought it was way over my head. Now I have a realistic idea of what it takes. It's a goal I want to work toward."

The decisions you make between the ages of nine and sixteen help you to shape your life as an adult. But they also help you make your life better *now.*

Glossary—*Explaining New Words*

birth control Methods for preventing pregnancy. These include "the pill," and condoms.
contraception Birth control.
cervix Lower, narrow end of the uterus that juts into the vagina.
fallopian tubes Two tubes that lead from the top of the uterus, one on each side. They carry the ripe eggs to the uterus.
follicle A tiny pocket in the ovary.
gynecologist A doctor who specializes in caring for female patients.

hormones Chemical substances that travel in your blood and tell your body organs how to develop. Your body makes hundreds of hormones. Estrogen and progesterone are the hormones that are linked with the menstrual cycle.

os Opening to the uterus.

ovaries Two organs the size and shape of almonds that provide safe storage for the thousands of eggs you were born with.

ovulation The process by which a ripe egg breaks out of its follicle and rises to the top of the ovary. Often (but not always) this is in the middle of your menstrual cycle.

menstrual cycle A 28-day cycle that includes actual menstruation (bleeding), the making of special hormones, the thickening of the uterine lining, ovulation, and the breakdown of the uterine lining.

pituitary gland Small oval gland near the brain.

puberty The period between the ages of nine and sixteen when girls and boys mature the most physically.

uterus Hollow organ that grows during puberty to the size of a clenched fist. The uterus can expand to many times its size. It is where a baby grows.

For Further Reading

Bell, Ruth. *Changing Bodies, Changing Lives: A Book for Teens on Sex and Relationships,* Revised and Updated, New York: Random House, 1988.

Boston Women's Health Book Collective. *The New Our Bodies, Ourselves.* New York: Simon & Schuster, Inc., 1984.

Brody, Jane, *Jane Brody's Nutrition Book.* New York: W.W. Norton, Inc., 1981.

Madaras, Lynda and Area, *The What's Happening To My Body? Book for Girls,* New Edition, New York: Newmarket Press, 1988.

Mahoney, Ellen Voelckers. *Now You've Got Your Period,* New York: Rosen Publishing Group, Inc., 1988.

Mucciolo, Gary. *Everything You Need to Know About Birth Control.* New York: Rosen Publishing Group, 1989.

Planned Parenthood. *How To Talk With Your Child About Sexuality.* New York: Doubleday & Company, Inc., 1986.

Index

About the Author

Ellen Kahaner is a freelance writer based in New York City. She has written a number of books for young adults and is currently at work on a series about groups of kids who are actively trying to improve life in their communities.

About the Editor

Evan Stark is a well-known sociologist, educator, and therapist—as well as a popular lecturer on women's and children's health issues. Dr. Stark was the Henry Rutgers Fellow at Rutgers University, and associate at the Institution for Social and Policy Studies at Yale University, and a Fulbright Fellow at the University of Essex. He is the author of many publications in the field of family relations and is the father of four children.

Acknowledgments and Photo Credits

Cover photo by Chuck Peterson

Photographs on pages 2,8, 27, 32, 42, 51, 55: Barbara Kirk; pages 14,20,31,49,59: Stuart Rabinowitz.

Art on pages 19, 24,37 by Sonja Kalter.

Design/Production: Blackbirch Graphics, Inc.

305.23

Kahaner, Ellen

Everything you
need to know
about growing up
female